Back in July 2018 Carol, my darling w   d active woman, suddenly suffered a probl

A normal evening, sitting together watching TV. She got up to leave the room, and turned to say something. (We later established she was telling me it was a repeat.) But what came out was not words, although it followed the pattern of a normal sentence, with intonation and stress. Just random sounds. For a brief second I thought she was pranking me, but even while she spoke her face changed. And we both realised something was seriously wrong.

A stroke would have been bad enough, but it was subsequently diagnosed as a brain tumour, a glioblastoma multiforme grade 4. It was centred around the region of the brain dealing with speech.

Treatment was an 'awake craniotomy', or debulking, intended to remove as much of the cancer as possible, conducted awake in an attempt to minimise damage to healthy brain tissue, and therefore the lowest possible impact on speech. Carol had no qualms. "Take out as much as you can". No hesitation. The team talked with Carol throughout the operation, her responses helping them to identify when they were close to critical areas and avoid them. You can't clearly see this type of cancer. It all looks the same. But it is vicious, spreading it's tentacles like a deadly octopus.

Carol declared herself very impressed with the process after the operation. Sadly though the prognosis was much less positive than we'd hoped, with an estimated 12 to 18 month timescale. When the swelling from the operation subsided we began a six week course of radiotherapy and chemotherapy, with a plan to follow on with a course of one week in four chemotherapy for a number of cycles.

Carol coped well with the initial six week course, although she disliked the tight-fitting mask necessary to fix her head in precise position for the radiotherapy. But she never flinched in her treatment. Despite suffering some marked physical deterioration, over the coming weeks she had three of the follow up courses of chemotherapy, before becoming too poorly to endure more. Over time she progressively lost the use of her right side. As a very active person this restriction on her mobility was a huge loss, and she was a very reluctant passenger in a wheelchair, although she still craved the opportunity to be outside.

But it was the effect on her speech and the increasing difficulty in finding the right words that she found most difficult. Carol was a founder member of the village choir, and had a beautiful singing voice. She tried very hard to rejoin them after the operation but the effects had been too great. Losing first the ability to sing, and then increasingly the ability to talk was devastating. Losing the ability to play with and talk to the granddaughters she loved so much was the worst loss of all. She also struggled terribly with the loss of her independence, but even more the impact on us. She didn't want to be a burden. She wasn't. I still struggle with the challenge she faced dealing with her forthcoming death, but robbed of the language to fully share her feelings and fears.

I was able to look after Carol at home until April. However when eventually her condition deteriorated beyond the point where I could safely look after her (unforgivably on my birthday) she was admitted to our local hospice on a respite basis. The intention was to bring her home when some issues had been resolved. The care and support we all received there was exemplary but sadly her condition deteriorated rapidly and she passed away in May, just 9 months after her first symptoms.

Throughout Carol's illness we were fortunate to enjoy the support of friends and family, and in the main, the NHS. I was also introduced to The Brain Tumour Charity's Carers Facebook group, people with loved ones with this vile disease, and experience of the whole Brain Tumour process, including those who had lost a loved one. They offered an online ear to listen to my fears and frustration, a shoulder to cry on when things got particularly tough, to offer advice and suggestions when sought, and a friendly non-judgmental environment in which I felt free to say what I wanted, when I wanted. As a carer sometimes you just need to rant, and ranting to friends and family can be counter productive and misconstrued. Often, in the wee small hours, I would post, and within minutes another carer somewhere around the world would respond. Because sleep was intermittent. And brain tumours know no boundaries.

From the start Carol's illness made conversation difficult. Partly that may have been the challenge that anyone must face when presented with a terminal prognosis; but in Carol's case further exacerbated by the cancer's effect on her language. Maybe I failed to encourage some of those most difficult conversations? Increasingly any conversation in her vicinity caused her distress, so over time lots of my thoughts and feelings went unspoken. I found myself writing more and more, sometimes in verse and sometimes prose, something I'd never done before. A few pieces I shared with that Facebook Group, and some members found they reflected their own thoughts and experiences and were helpful. Looking back on it now each piece reflects different stages in our journey, and brings those memories back forcefully. Some hurt much more now than they did when I wrote them. Some seem irrelevant. They were undoubtedly cathartic for me, and helped maintain my sanity.

Together they reflect much more honestly the way things felt than this somewhat emotionless introduction. Reading back through them the majority are about dealing with the aftermath. In my mind I had thought I had written more during Carol's illness. Maybe I should have.

Emotions change over time. Some pieces are quite bleak. Some more optimistic. Some realistic. It's not a straight line, grief. Up and down. One step forward, two steps back.

So having shared the spoiler that things did not end well, you may want to think twice before reading on. If you want to continue then I am happy to share with you. I'm sorry if they're self-obsessed, but I'm afraid I have been.

Some of the pieces make me proud. Some ashamed. But that's sadly just the truth of situations like this. No-one can ever get it right.

To academics and purists I apologise for my poetry. You may not appreciate the fact these poems (usually, almost) rhyme and scan. Too old school for many. But these were not academic pieces, not pretending to be literature. Just me trying to capture the emotions that were otherwise trapped inside. For some reason rhyme helped me overcome the fiercely personal emotion they represent. Without exception each piece came to me pretty much fully formed as I lay awake in the middle of the night, or sat alone beside Carol's bed. I may have tweaked some a tad in the cold light of day, but I have always remained true to the original.

Too many of us are forced into a carer's role at some stage in out lives. Wherever you are on your own journey some of it may strike true. Until you've been there you can't understand the issues. I wish you and your loved ones every good fortune. And if you are affected by similar circumstances you may find it of some limited reassurance to know that others have been where you are now.

Brain tumours are poorly understood and research severely under funded. Too many people suffer. That suffering is unbearable.

Thank you for buying the book. All royalties I receive will go to the Brain Tumour Charity.

I hope you will find the book of some comfort. I hope you will share the details with friends and family. And if you do find it helpful, please leave a review.

If you would like to make a donation to the Brain Tumour Charity, I have set up a JustGiving page, and any donations made there in Carol's memory will go direct to them. Please use the link below.

https://bit.ly/3bRcci5

Thank you.
From me. From The Brain Tumour Charity. And from Carol.

Taxi

Written in the days immediately after the diagnosis,
with optimism and hope.

Leaving this party early? So they say.
Await death's taxi horn to summon you away?
How could you leave us if you cared?
For joy is only there when shared.
All the grand things we might in future see,
Will be as nought without you there with me.

And I am weak, and you are strong,
How will I cope when you are gone?
Solid together, yet so weak alone,
You are the mortar to my stone.
And those who know us, they could always see,
Me just the shadow to your sun-drenched tree.

The risk to you is huge, and yet,
That's not for you the most important threat.
A gaping hole in lives you shaped and steered,
The tragic loss for them is what you've feared.

But you are me, and I am you,
It's who we are, it's what we do.
We'll fight this blasted thing together.
Fight it now. Fight on forever.

Mixed feelings now on fate's cruel intervention,
A joyful life must be our best intention.
Woken from my complacency,
To realise too late just what you mean to me.
Time to be truly close again,
However long or short that may remain.

Doing things planned but never done,
Extracting every ounce of fun.
Laugh even more than I recall,
Just holding hands on seaside wall.
Watch crimson sunsets in the night,
With ice cream cones in dwindling light.

So taxi let your meter run,
We will not leave 'til we are done.
We know one day you'll be outside,
Eventually we all must take that ride.

But we'll fight on, keep you away,
Together every single day.
Hoping your taxi won't arrive,
But knowing none escape this world alive.

Let's be honest
Written as we struggled coming to terms with the reality.

When we got that diagnosis, on that God forsaken day,
When they told us that your tumour would soon carry you away,
We determined to be positive and fight it to the end,
Eking every bit of pleasure out of every day we spend.

But the life we live's not real now, we're just acting out a lie.
We are feigning false contentment, 'cos we're just too brave to cry.
Acting out this cheerful subterfuge is driving me insane,
Our energy all wasted, saving others from our pain.

We hide the fear and hurt that is boiling up inside us,
"Don't bother others now dear, oh, please don't make a fuss."
As soon as the front door closes though we're snapping at each other.
How are we meant to cope when our true feelings we just smother?

I wanted it so perfect, these last months we'd spend together,
Aligned to face the emptiness bearing down on us forever.
Not fighting with each other over meals I've poorly cooked,
Or complaints that I should take more care about the way I looked.

The days for me are stuffed brim full of loveless, trivial tasks,
"Have you cleaned the kitchen floor again?" repeatedly you ask.
This time was meant to help us grow ever more close together,
Before that desperate day ahead that splits us up forever.

Instead though I'm becoming a browbeaten, grumpy cleaner,
An ill equipped old skivvy who's emotionally meaner.
I can't allow this way to be our build up to "goodbye",
With resentment, yes, and anger, even relief behind my eye.

I love you still my darling, more than you will ever know,
I hate you still for leaving, and I pray that you won't go.
I'm terrified of what's to come, not knowing if I'll cope,
Be brave enough to soldier on when slipping down that slope.

I must rise up above them, all these galling, trivial things,
Remember now the heartfelt joy your love for me still brings.
Whatever pain is crippling me, for you it's so much worse,
The pain for you is physical, I hide in prose and verse.

I know your wish that when you're gone that I must somehow cope,
You know how hard that that will be when you're my source of hope.
So please forgive me darling, I'm just selfish now and weak,
Emotion saved for written words of which we'll never speak.

I'll bite my tongue, and think how much I know I'll always love you,
My job now just to ease your leaving in whatever ways I can do.

On thin ice
Written when I felt overwhelmed and ill equipped for my role as carer.

In my dream, I wake. My eyes still closed I feel the cold.

I look around, and I am standing on a sea of ice; no landmarks, just ice stretching to the horizon in every direction. I am not properly equipped. Bare feet where there should be warm boots. A thin jumper not a fur filled parka. Beside me my precious cargo.

And then I notice that my feet are wet. The ice beneath us is melting. "Keep moving" comes the call, as another ill-dressed carer pushes past.

And so another day begins. I slither and stumble, pushing my beloved who knows where. Her weight shifts, so our direction changes, but since we have no real destination it matters not.

What will it be like when we finally arrive? I hate the journey, but I fear that final crack in the ice so much more.

Contrasts
*Written on a bright spring morning, with Carol smiling,
appreciating the good days.*

Just like the weather today my darling wife was sparkling. Perhaps it's the
contrast; the bleaker the day before, the more glorious the warmth of the sun and
the smile on her face today.

It doesn't take much to make me happy these days. What I'd give for more days
of sunshine and smiles. Wishing everyone a sunny, smiley day.

Kidnapped
Written after being deeply hurt by something Carol had said.

Taking care of my wife is an honour. To think that the things I do can give her comfort and relief and companionship to help her deal with an impossibly daunting prognosis is a privilege.

But the person I care for some days is not my wife. She has been kidnapped by an insurgent who is holding her hostage.

I can't free her from her prison. Attempts to kill her captor have failed. So I must endure a future where I care for them both. Too often now I only see her captor. He can be sullen and rude, and is certainly demanding.

But I know, hidden away from me, my darling wife knows it's her I'm caring for. Sometimes, increasingly rarely, I see her. "I love you. Thank you for looking after me". So I try to remember that sentence when things get tough, even when she's hidden from me, and look past the selfish, murderous terrorist who has stolen both our lives.

Undelete

Written on the first night after Carol slipped into the last phase.

My darling is safe and calm at the hospice. We know things are moving forward now towards an end we hoped would never come.

Doctors have advised us to pace ourselves for what might still be some weeks away. That means I'm at home for a shower and a proper night's sleep. The Sky box is on and I'm selecting which recordings are 'me' recordings, and which are 'us' recordings.

I watched an 'us' recording almost without thinking, deleted it, then undeleted it and pressed the 'keep' button.

And then wondered why. I know Carol will never come home again. And now I'm wondering whether I'll want to watch 'us' programs any more. 'Us' programs are ones to share. To enjoy together. Ones where Carol can remind me of character's names and relationships. Who did what to whom. Ones where she would want to know what happened more than me.

What happens to 'us' stuff now?

Deafening silence
Written in the long hours spent beside Carol's bed in the Hospice.

In these last fading moments, as you wait to take your leave,
I'm sitting here beside you and I'm learning how to grieve.
The demands of your foul tumour mean you struggle now with sound,
And I struggle with the silence since unspoken words abound.

So I'll write them down instead my love, the things I want to say,
But most of it is no surprise, I think it everyday.
I love you more than life itself, you are the best of me,
A future that's without you there, a barren destiny.

So many hours in recent months we've been so close together,
But those are not the memories that I could ever treasure,
Think back instead to when we met, the feelings that it stirred,
I think you barely noticed me, my antics so absurd.

But slowly I got through to you and broke your world apart,
When finally I found a way to sneak inside your heart.
I've loved you every day since then, so grateful that we met,
The children that you raised so well to make things better yet.

And grandchildren who came along and crammed out lives with joy,
So many happy hours with them that we got to enjoy.
But now there's things you'll never see, not watch them grow and thrive,
How much richer their growing up if you were still alive.

I'll do my best to share with them the love you would have given,
For things I miss that you would not, I hope I am forgiven.
Now even in your leaving dear you've shown great dignity,
So proud to share my life with you, and I hope you with me.

There's many loved ones left behind, and floods of tears will fall.
The gaping holes you leave behind the saddest thing of all.
But now "Goodbye my love" I mouth, it's time for you to go.
And all our love it goes with you, but that I think you know.

What you taught me
Written in the hospice late one night, close to the end.

When the final golden sunset sees you stolen from this earth,
When the world is robbed forever of your love and care and mirth,
I must remember when you're missing, when I turn around for you,
That your soul lives on forever in the hearts of all you knew.

Try to recall the things I learned from you, throughout our happy years,
And do my best to live that life, not lose myself in tears.
To be kind and fair and honest, tolerant of other's faults,
To be patient and compassionate, and other things you taught.

I'll think about you always, think about what you would do,
And try to raise a smile, not tear, whenever thoughts may turn to you.
For in truth you'll never leave me, you'll be with me 'til my end,
Making me a better person, always there as my best friend.

Dagger of Guilt

Written in the days immediately following Carol's death, full of guilt.

I've a dagger pushed inside me, on its handle is carved 'Guilt',
Its serrated blade is burning, separated from its hilt.
No way to pull it out now, and no way to ease the pain,
No way to ease the hurting, just so hard to smile again.
So many ways I failed you, how I let you down it seems,
And held you back from chasing all your precious, long held dreams.
Thought you loved me like I loved you, thought that you were happy too,
Were your words when leaving honest, were they really, really true?

What do I mourn?

Written in the weeks following Carol's death.

I can't be sure just what I mourn,
What loss now leaves me so forlorn?
It's not the warrior gone at last,
Your days of fighting on had passed.
And not the glorious girl I wed,
For months ago I knew her dead.
Not me, the carer day and night,
Relieved no more to fight that fight.

I think perhaps it's me I've lost,
Into life's mix alone now tossed.
I'm ill equipped to find my way,
I don't know what to think, or say.
No guiding hand now there to lead me,
I don't know who or what I can be.
Where do I even want to go?
Who do I even want to know?

No longer husband to my wife,
But some new independent life.
It's me I mourn, it's me I miss,
An empty shell, not fit for this.
Where once there was both joy and laughter,
There's trudging on, today and after.
Though those I love have rallied too,
Including me in what they do,

And though I'm loved and welcome there,
No longer half our lifelong pair.
The one who didn't need my words,
Just understood when things occurred.
You always knew just what I thought,
And made me do the things I ought.
Without you there, there is no me,
A shadow where you ought to be.
Go through the motions, carry on,
But what's the point now you are gone?

Little things
Recognising that it's the small things that can hurt the most.

It's not the anniversary,
That knocks the stuffing out of me,
For those big dates I can prepare,
I brace myself 'cos you're not there.

It's little things that catch me out,
Everyday things out and about.
A favourite taste or simple smell,
A piece of music works as well.

Trivial things are so much harder,
Unopened treats hid in the larder,
With use-by dates a long time past,
But you bought them, so they stay fast.

Facebook reminders, "Five years on",
Some message sent when you weren't gone.
And in the garden your pink rose,
It's colour pure, scent fills my nose.

I pruned it wrong before you left,
And though it's blooming I'm bereft.
But somehow it's a comfort too,
So many things that just mean 'you',

Reminding me of what we had,
Reminding me I should be glad.
So lucky you were in my life,
So proud to have you as my wife.

Covering up

Thinking about the things I did or didn't do.

Just put it out of your mind.
But you don't.
You maybe just take if off the day to day agenda.
Add it to the list of things you don't discuss with anyone.
But inside you think about them all the time.

Layers
Recognising that my bereavement may be hard for others to deal with.

"How are you doing" people ask,
"This grieving process such a task."
"How do you think you're getting on?"
(Now half your life is dead and gone?)

Replies they don't come readily,
No simple answer can there be.
But now a little time's gone by,
I think I understand more why.

The superficial layer's fine,
The pain is now almost benign.
I can now think of you and smile,
With happy memories for a while.

I celebrate the life we knew,
Instead of cursing losing you.
That's layer one of grief I guess,
Improvements there I will confess.

But there are other layers too,
Affect this new life without you.
The menial, the 'how do I?'
Expose new tasks as days go by.

Though jobs were shared, we always knew,
Some fell to me, some fell to you.
Washing machines, home schedules too.
What should I cook? Clean up? Rinse through?

Stock up on greetings cards ahead,
And Christmas plans all neat instead.
Eventually those things I'll master,
Though you did better and much faster.

But underneath this trivial list,
The deepest layer sorely missed,
To never have you next to me,
To be as close as two can be.

To feel your love and know it true,
To trust someone in all you do.
Someone who knew your inner soul,
The good, the bad, they loved the whole.

For that, my love, is gone forever,
Built from a lifetime spent together.
But no-one else will understand,
The pain of reaching for your hand.

And no-one else can share that pain,
Though they may ask me yet again.
And when they ask me "How are you?"
Which layer should I answer to?

Not 'I' but 'we'

Recognising that some words I still use have special meaning.

Funny it's still not 'I' but 'we',
Still 'ours' not 'mine', indefinitely,
For you are gone, you're floating free,
But I know you're still next to me,
And always will be.

Christmas

Approaching the first Christmas, Carol's special time.

It's "Season's greetings" so we say,
Though some we love have gone away.
They've left us lonely on our own,
Emotions felt but not quite shown.

This time of year you did enjoy,
Filled it with love for girl and boy.
We always looked to you for fun,
But with you gone has it begun?

I need to stand and do my part,
Although your absence breaks my heart.
I must remember your last year,
Determination showing clear.

That we'd remember this with love,
Though now you're taken up above.
For Christmas, dear, will always be,
Your love for all our family.

Carer's lament

Written a month after Carol died, recognising the unfairness of the guilt shared by so many carers.

At last your carer's duty's done, with loved one gone like setting sun.
New things now open up for you, some welcome, some you're forced to do.
You must unlock emotion's door, behind which things are red and raw.
You'll start with sadness at your loss, mixed with relief that caring's dross,
And heartless tasks have ended too, caring for them so hard to do.
And anger too that fate should choose, the two of you, life's game to lose.
"Why us" you cry, "why pick on us? Why did you have to treat us thus?"
"Was treatment all it could have been? There were new drugs, new things I've
seen."

And now dread Guilt may start to come, in questioning each thing you'd done,
You challenge every single choice, with Guilt's loud and persistent voice.
Every past thought, act and omission, exposed for criticism and revision.
"Did I seek help quite soon enough? Was I too gentle, or too rough?"
"Was patience not all it could be? Did I just think too much of me?"

You have to challenge Guilt's attack, unreasoned and unhealthy flak.
You know you did your very best, you loved, and cared and they were blessed,
To have you fighting by their side, you carried on and tried and tried.
Impossible the task you faced, that caring role upon you placed.
You know you did all you could do, all carers send respect to you.
So focus now on what was good, where you'd return to if you could.
Just look back to the days of old, the happy days, pre carer's role.
Remember now the one you love, let that fine image rise above,
And push the guilt and grief away, good now the memory each day.
So let the mourning stage begin, let overwhelming sadness in.
Accepting now that they are gone, a life without them moving on.
Reshape your life around that hole, they've left inside your very soul.
And realise your hardest task, harder than anyone should ask,
Is how your life you'll now rebuild, without the one who once it filled.
Accepting that some days are sad, some very good, some very bad.

But always keep the thought with you,
That you did all that you could do.

Loving by rote

Written after realising you can get into the habit of grief.

When we're young, much of what we learn is achieved through simple repetition; the alphabet, our times tables. Repeated often enough those things become fixed into our minds and we barely need to think of them. They're just there.

In much the same way, those we love fix themselves in our minds and hearts. They're a constant, and every day we spend with them reinforces our love.

But when they are snatched away from us, and we lose that constant reinforcement, that permanence and certainty can be challenged. Guilt and sadness and anger and a raft of other emotions temporarily overwhelm that loving certainty, flooding our lives with negativity.

Hard as it may be we must strive not to allow those negative thoughts to dominate too much and too often, for fear that, by rote, those new, negative emotions become fixed in our heart and mind and overwhelm the positive memories we should instead treasure forever.

What would Nana say?

Written as I faced up to trying to fill Carol's grandmother role.

We miss you Carol every day,
We miss you more than we can say.
I try my best to push on through,
Our granddaughters they all miss you,
I try to fill the boots you'd fill.
A poor replacement yes, but still.
Using your name when with them too,
I try applying what you knew,
To problems that they let show through,
There's added weight to 'words from you'.
"Well Nana would have said" I say,
And hope your thoughts I might convey.
For anything that's linked to you,
Has added value, "Sure it's true!".
So even though you're far away,
You guide us all upon our way.

Angel's wishes

Remembering Carol's instructions to me, that I should try to be happy.

So when your Angel's looking down,
Don't let them see you always frown.
Although they're gone, their love's still true,
It's happiness they want for you.

They do not want your life to stop,
And when they witness each tear drop,
They urge you on to better things,
And sometimes you may feel their wings.

You'll always feel their heart-felt loss,
The pain too sharp to over gloss.
Imagine though, reversed the roles,
If you were gone and they were whole.

What would you want if fate allowed?
You'd want them happy, true and bold.

Never

Accepting the permanence of this changed condition.

I don't think I truly understood the infinite, permanent significance of 'never'
before.
Never hold your hand again.
Never watch the dawn together.
Never hear your laugh, or see your smiling face.

Never forget you.

Anniversary

Facing up to that first anniversary of Carol's death and exactly one year later the first Covid lockdown.

Sometimes I just cannot believe,
You're gone, I'm left and still I grieve.
Last painful months that we went through,
That left me lost here without you.

You were the very best of me,
As all around us then could see.
I lost my life's deliverance,
I lost my one most blessed chance.

And now I have to live like this,
What I would give for one more kiss.
For you've been gone now one full year,
Time-frame distorted by my tears.

I thought that I'd begun to cope,
But lock-down has destroyed that hope.
I'm trapped inside, feel on the brink.
About you, all the time I think.

If you were here you'd keep me sane,
You'd have me up as right as rain.
We'd laugh and joke, we'd play the fool,
But now instead I know that you'll,
Be looking down, be cross with me,
For giving up so readily.
Self pity fills my waking hours,
My resolution elsewhere cowers.

One year on
Realising how time has been distorted over the last months.

It seems untrue 12 months have passed,
Time went so slow, time went so fast.
Timescale corrupted by grief's tears,
It felt like days, it felt like years.
Now more than ever I love you,
Asking myself what would you do?
Now lock-down's here to change the game,
No 'normal' will there be again.
For without you here there's no such word,
'Different' perhaps, 'new' is assured.
But those who love you carry on,
Smile when we can, though you are gone.
Remembering the love you gave,
Remembering how you were brave.
Your memory a shining light,
My lighthouse in the darkest night.

Love you Carol

The hole in the whole of your life.
Taking a different perspective on loss.

When you lose someone so precious, someone who has been such a huge part of who you are, it's impossibly hard.

Their absence is not like any absence you've experienced before. In fact to describe their loss as an absence is misleading. Instead there is instead rather a presence beside you, albeit a terrifying black hole that sucks your happiness into itself. Anti-matter.

For some time that hole in your life is toxic. Something to be avoided or denied. People round you may get a sense of it. Some will avoid getting too close for fear of being drawn into it; a few seem immune to the gravitational pull and will provide much needed support.

We waste a lot of time hoping that the hole will somehow close up. Heal itself. Disappear.
But over time we begin to accept that the hole is a permanent presence inside us. And when we accept it as a lifelong companion it loses some of its terrors. We learn we can look into the schism, and deep inside see through the sadness to some of the happiness we thought we'd lost forever. Memories of happy times. Reminders of the things most precious.

You may be gone, but you're with me forever.

Spain
Questioning whether to hold on to our holiday home.

When we went there first it was nothing. But you saw the potential. You saw a future.
I grew to love it, perhaps even more than you.

Eventually I think you craved more. And I held you back. You the sail. Me the anchor. I was just happy to be with you.

And now you're gone I don't know what I feel.

The stress of getting here, but the total relaxation when I arrive.

It's not the same. But then nothing is the same. The gap in my life is perhaps more exaggerated here than at home. When we were here it was just us. Together 24/7 for as long as we stayed. So now, in contrast, it's just me. I look at the same sights, visit the same places. I love them still. But I loved them more when we shared them. And your absence is somehow even more obvious here than at home. More intense.

Decision time. Is it better to enjoy what I can, and bear the pain of you not being here? Or to say goodbye and sidestep the pain?

If only you could tell me.

Lonely in a crowd
Feeling lonely.

It's not being with people that stops you feeling lonely.
Loneliness is missing that one person who has gone forever.

Until
Missing Carol, but feeling her near.

You are beside me when I wake every morning, until I open my eyes.
You are with me through every day, until I reach for your hand.
You are at my side for every challenge I face, until I ask you to speak.
You are my constant companion, until I turn to look at you.
You will be with me forever, until the day I die.

Unopened doors
The confusion of grief.

I think of my brain like a jumble of corridors, with doors leading off to different 'rooms'. The doors are labelled. Things like "Shopping" or "Gardening" or "Maintenance".

Since bereavement the doors are still there, but now they seem more randomly organised. To be honest, I'm not sure I knew what was behind some of them before, or where they were or that they even existed. They were Carol's doors.

I've managed to find most of them now, albeit not always as frequently as I should, and I'm slowly becoming accustomed to the new layout.

But there are some doors I still struggle to open.
"Memories of the bad times".
"Memories of the good times".

Indeed, for a while I kept those doors locked as best I could.

And when I do open one of those difficult doors, in an attempt to sort through the contents and tidy, they all seem to be interconnected, so as I sneak inside all the other doors fly open. And then I lose control. My mind flies randomly through those rooms, not stopping in any one long enough to look thoroughly at what's inside, or have a chance to tidy up.

I guess all the doors are always linked in some way. And maybe that 'out of control' feeling is getting less frequent. But I still tend to open some of those doors carefully.

I remember
Written when thoughts passed back to earlier times.

When you first came into my life, I'd no idea you'd be my wife,
But how I liked the look of you, the things you'd say, the things you'd do.
But we were wed to others then, and so I wondered if or when.

But sometimes I would catch your eye, reluctant smiles disdain belied.
More frequent then our eyes would meet, sometimes we'd walk out in the street,
To share a coffee or a snack, to laugh and talk, but then go back,
To partners waiting safe at home, who'd no idea that we might roam.

We'd no intent to cause them pain, but gradually too great the strain,
Of falling deep in love together, breaking vows that bind forever,
Leaving old spouses in the past, together with new love at last.

Then children came to build our joy, second a girl, but first a boy,
And you took on that caring role, and guided them towards our goal,
Of people of whom we'd be proud, whose qualities we'd shout aloud.
I knew I was, from our first date, punching so far above my weight,
Whatever could be wrong with you, that my facade you'd not see through?

You stuck with me through good and bad, through all the happy times and sad,
When I was ill you cared for me, though nurse not what you'd choose to be,
But even so you'd see me right, until I'd have another fright.
And all that time I held you back, "I can't do this, we can't do that".
We both assumed I'd be the first, to have my earthly bubble burst,
And you would then be free to grow, to sing and dance, go to that show.

But cancer had not read the script, that blossoming performance ripped,
Instead foul tumour stole your brain, a wondrous life not lived in vain,
But cruelly stolen at the last, your loved ones stunned and left aghast,
That someone so alive as you, should lose the future you were due.

I love you dear with all my heart, I cannot bear to be apart,
But how I love your legacy, the family you gave to me,
The attitudes that you held true, everything else I owe to you.

Yet sometimes I can't help but cry, I never want to say "goodbye".

On your own

Coming to terms with being alone.

On your own; it's safer.
No risk; no threat. Do it your way.
On your own; it's quicker. No waiting for confirmation. No debate.
On your own; it's empty.
No value. No reason.
On your own.
Always. On your own.

Eclipse
Trying to understand what's going on in my head and heart.

I spend a lot of time thinking about my feelings. Some might say it's better to just let your feelings come rather than picking at them, but I find it helps me to try to understand what's going on inside my head and heart. So here's my theory on learning to live with grief. My grief. Of course I can't speak for anyone else.

Before Carol's illness my world, like everyone's I'm assuming, contained lots of different emotions. Love of close friends and family; the warmth of friendship; irritation with some; antipathy towards a few. Excitement about some new things, trepidation about others. If I'm honest a bit of envy here and there. But the important point is those emotions all co-existed simultaneously, and always with the capacity for new emotions to be added – the arrival of a new grandchild for example. I didn't need to stop loving someone else to love the newcomer. And just because I might not see some of my loved ones very often I didn't love them less.

Carol's illness and death changed that. Her loss was so immense it was like a total eclipse of my emotional sun. An overwhelming darkness. And just as early man must have looked at an eclipse and thought the sun was gone forever, so for me all other emotions had disappeared, subsumed by that one desperate sadness. Like an eclipse the process was (still is) gradual. Initially a lack of all emotion. A greyness. Then overwhelming sadness, blocking out all those old emotions. Only able to feel that darkness, that one emotion of grief.

But then, as the eclipse slowly progresses and a little light returns, with it the return of small pleasures. And for me that is almost the hardest thing. Feeling guilty when I let that sadness slip.
As if I'm being disloyal.

Part of me hopes that when the eclipse finally ends that pain will be gone. But I know it won't.
Although there is a chink of light.

I think perhaps the concept of learning to live with grief is being able to return to that previous world of multiple emotions co-existing, where all my previous emotions are allowed to reappear from behind the shadow. Except with the addition of those most important new elements: the treasured memories of my darling in happier times; the immense sadness at the permanence of her loss. Even the sad memories of her decline that I still try so hard to forget.

Accepting that I can love her, and hate her for going, and miss her all at the same time.

And finally the recognition of me as an individual, with all that may bring. Allowing space for the addition of new experiences and happiness when (if) they come.

Yes for me that's my goal. To get to a situation where I can accept that. I'm still a long way off, but I think I might be moving in the right direction. Whether I get there or not only time will tell.

Scuttling things

Trying to move on.

Emotions roller coaster calms, weeping and sadness healing balms,
The gaping wound begins to heel, the loss something you'll always feel.

Yet days will come again to smile, pain locked away for just a while.
You start to think of a new you, a different life to that you knew.

Not leaving memories behind, but moving on, just to be kind.
Stumble along life's pebbled path, disturbing rocks the aftermath.

And under some lie scuttling things, those hidden thoughts, your guilt begins.
Those images may gain control, confusing feelings take their toll.

But standing still you must not do, avoiding risks that upset you.
The choice is not an 'either or', just mourning all that went before.

Make do with half the life we knew, or start again, build life anew,
Never forget the love we lost, impossible, too great a cost.

But rather mix both then and now, merging the past and future how,
To build a life to live again, still missing you, but easing pain.

Adaptation
Starting to move forward.

I think I'm learning to live without you.

I don't like it much, but I think I'm beginning to adapt.

At the start I only wanted to do the same things we always did, because *we* did them. And that meant your absence was always there. It was almost as if I was walking those old roads hoping to bump into you. I didn't of course, but that didn't stop me looking. Sadly that fruitless search just made things worse.

I didn't want to change anything, because that felt like I might erase a part of you, make your memory a bit less distinct.

Now, for the first time I'm realising that I *can* (or maybe even *must*) do different things, or not do the old things, and there is not the tiniest chance my memory of you will be reduced.

That's what I think living will be now. Doing things Ive been avoiding. Not doing things Ive done through habit. When it feels right.

Moving furniture from where you liked it (even if I will undoubtedly move it back again).

Walking around the marina in Spain and sitting making up my own stories about the beautiful yachts and their owners.

Getting up late (or early).

Painting and drawing into the small hours, or not for weeks.

You're always with me. I hope you like where we're going now.

Printed in Great Britain
by Amazon

79678619R00031